The Joy of Ragtime

Selected and edited by Denes Agay

In April 1896 Tony Pastor's Music Hall in New York—a legendary showcase for many famous entertainers of the day—advertised the appearance of "Ben R. Harney, author, musician and comedian; originator of the only absolute novelty in this season's vaudevilles; piano playing in syncopated or 'rag time', singing his own melodies and doing his original dancing." The act was an instantaneous hit; ragtime and cake walk swept the country and became a national craze.

To be historically accurate, Ben Harney was not the "originator" of this excitingly new style of popular piano music. For numerous years before him Negro pianists, including the immensely gifted Scott Joplin, had been playing ragtime piano in various Midwestern honky-tonk cafes and waterfront saloons. Harney merely exposed ragtime to American audiences at large; through him it received respectability, and enthusiastic acceptance.

Ragtime is characterized by a strongly syncopated melody in the treble against a steady, regularly accented accompaniment in the left hand. The form is adapted from the 19th century instrumental dance patterns, the march, the polka, and the quadrille: a sequence of four or five sixteen-measure sections, each repeated, with an occasional reprise of the main theme. Into this traditional European mold the foremost creators of ragtime piano music, Scott Joplin, James Scott, Joseph F. Lamb and a few others, were able to infuse so much melodic originality and rhythmic vitality, that through them, ragtime became an indigenous, beguiling American idiom, one of the main sources of jazz.

The Joy of Ragtime includes the best and most durable examples of this unique musical heritage in an approximately graded sequence. The works are in their original forms, unless it is indicated that they were edited or arranged. Some simplified rags appear in the first half of the volume to furnish a repertory of appealing solos for the easy grades.

The music in this collection covers the golden age of ragtime, 1896 through 1917. Its current renaissance firmly and joyously attests to ragtime's indestructibility and its solid musical values.

Denes Agay

© Yorktown Music Press, Inc. 1974
33 West 60th Street, New York 10023

Music Sales Limited, 78 Newman Street, W1 London

International Standard Book Number 0-8256-8016-6
Library of Congress Card Catalogue Number 74-83440

Contents

Cakewalk Parade

1. Fly, You Blackbirds

Arranged by Denes Agay

From Brainard's
Ragtime Collection
(1899)

Moderately lively

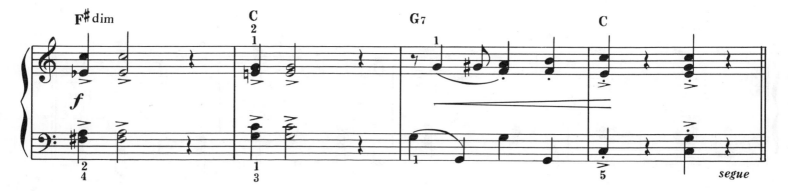

segue

2. Mississippi Rag

W. H. Krell

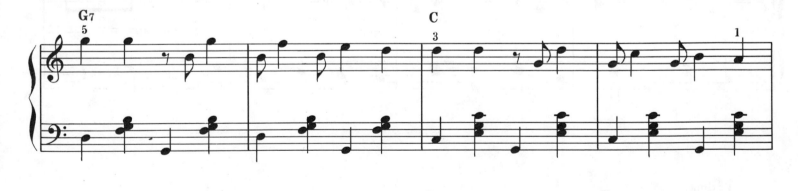
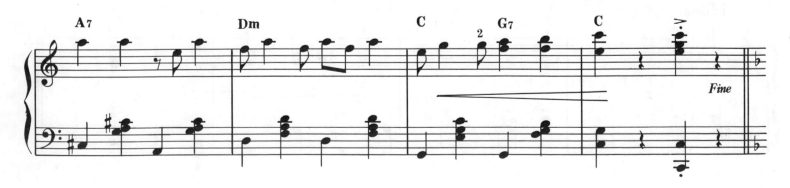

3. Smoky Mokes

Abe Holzman

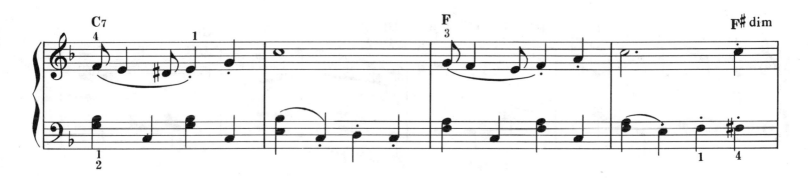

Repeat Nos. 1 and 2

The Entertainer

A Ragtime Two-Step

Simplified arrangement by Denes Agay

Scott Joplin

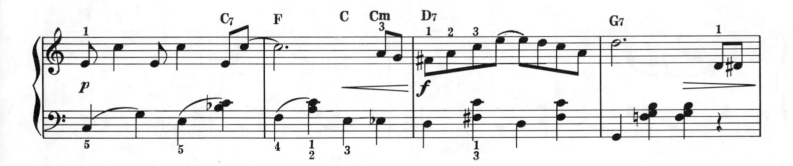

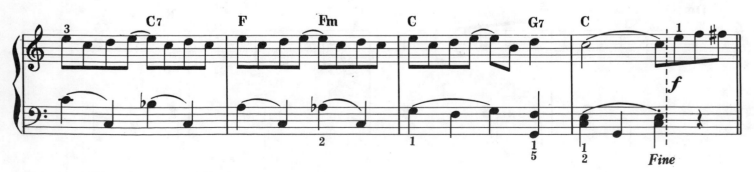

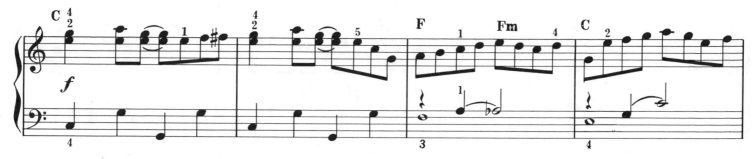

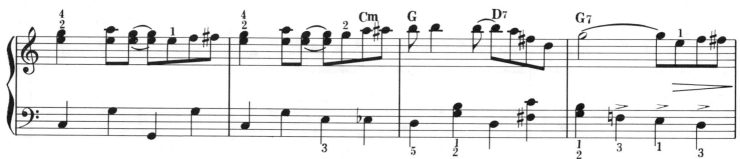

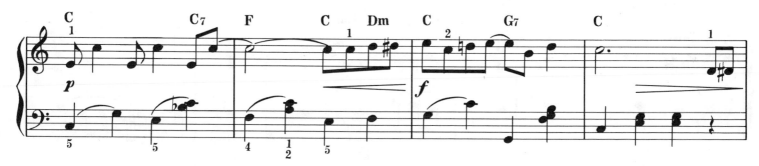

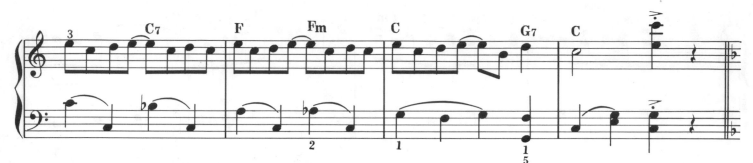

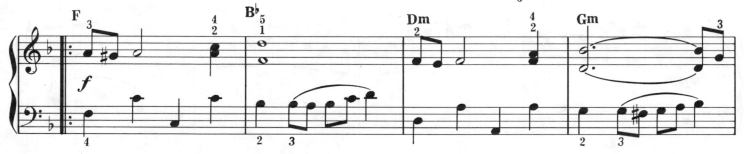

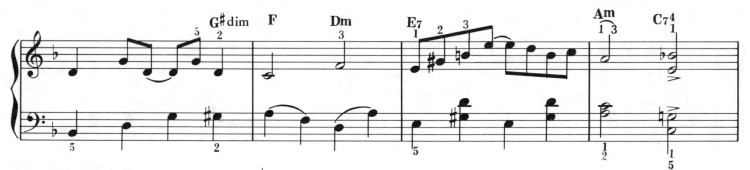

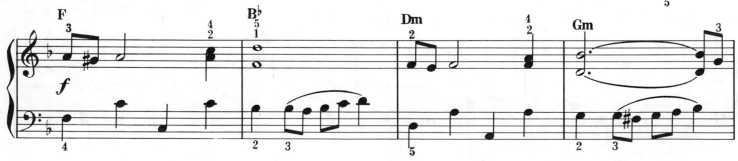

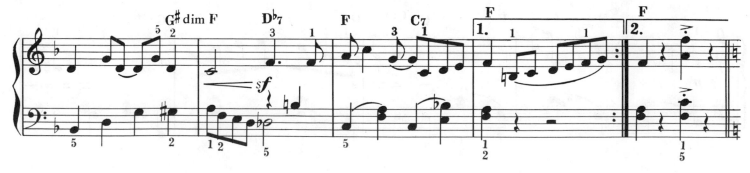

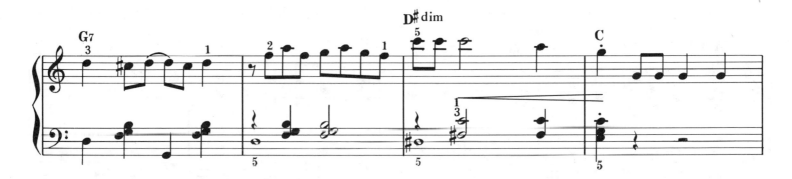

D.C. al Fine

The Bos'n Rag

Moderate march tempo

Fred S. Stone

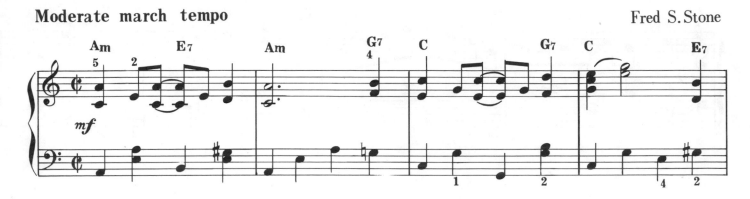

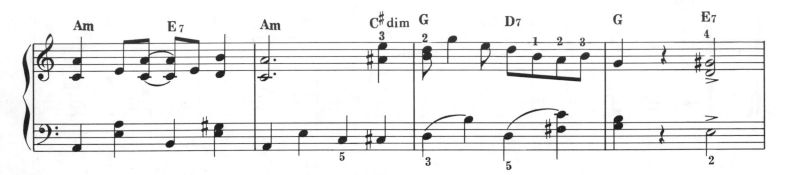

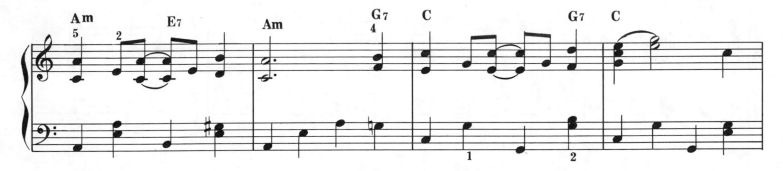

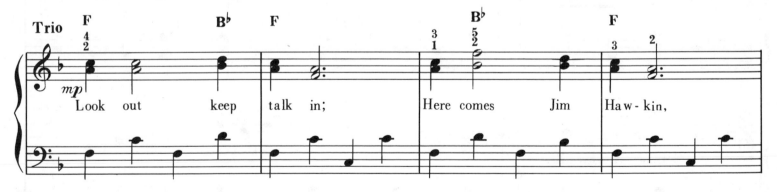

Look out keep talk in; Here comes Jim Haw- kin,

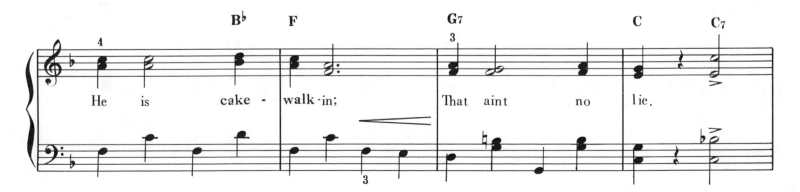

He is cake - walk -in; That aint no lie.

Old folks a - watch - in , Young-n's a - march - in' For they'll

win that ere cake or die.

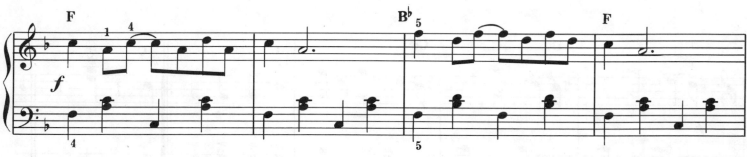

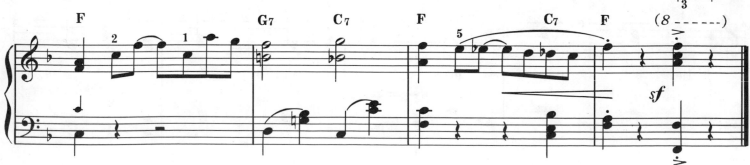

Ragtime Song Fest

1. Hello, Ma Baby

Howard and Emerson

Lively Cakewalk

Hel-lo! ma ba-by, Hel-lo! ma hon-ey, Hel-lo! ma rag-time gal,

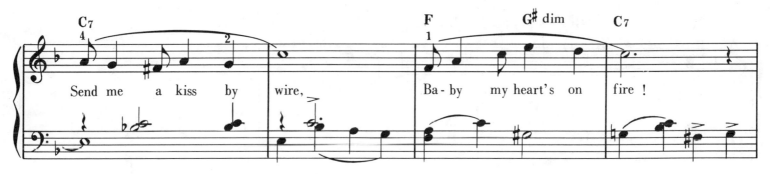

Send me a kiss by wire, Ba-by my heart's on fire!

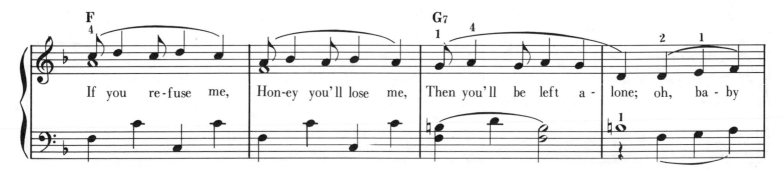

If you re-fuse me, Hon-ey you'll lose me, Then you'll be left a-lone; oh, ba-by

tel-e-phone and tell me I'se your own.

segue

2. Mister Johnson, Turn Me Loose

Ben Harney

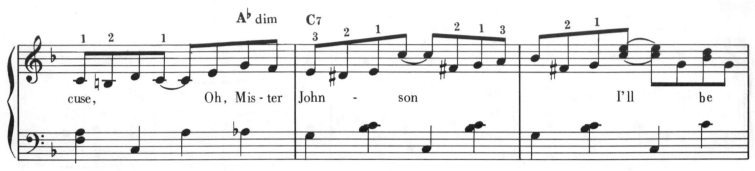

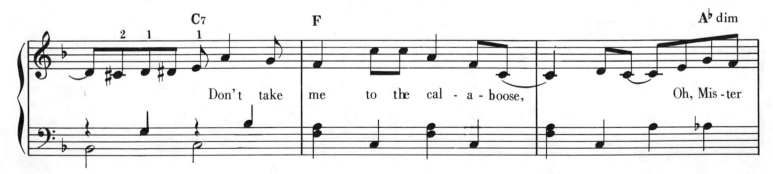

segue

3. Rufus, Rastus, Johnson Brown

Von Tilzer — Sterling

Ru - fus, Ras - tus, John - son Brown what you goin to do when the

rent comes round, What you going to say, how you goin' to pay, You'll

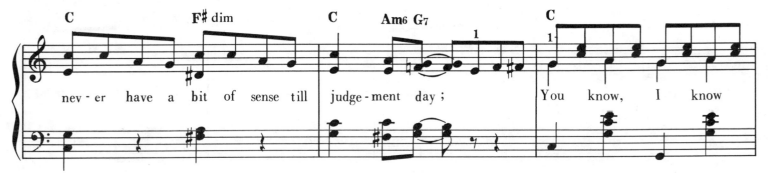

nev - er have a bit of sense till judge - ment day; You know, I know

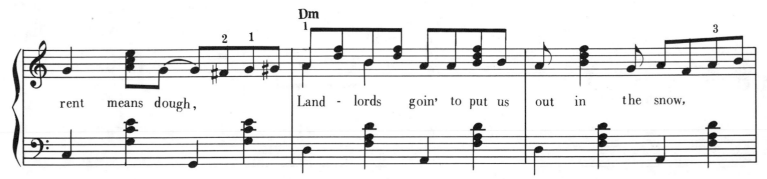

rent means dough, Land - lords goin' to put us out in the snow,

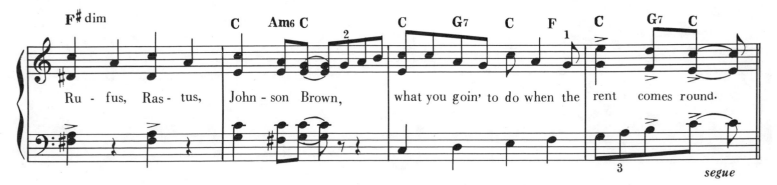

Ru - fus, Ras - tus, John - son Brown, what you goin' to do when the rent comes round.

segue

4. Living a Ragtime Life

Roberts-Jefferson

I got a rag time dog and a rag - time cat, A rag - time pi - a - no in my

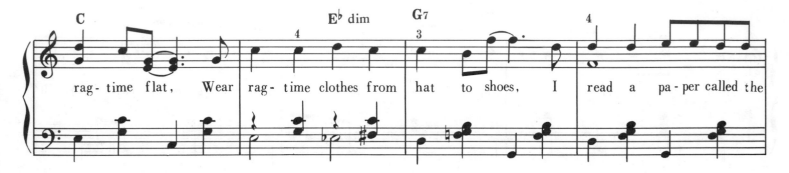

rag - time flat, Wear rag - time clothes from hat to shoes, I read a pa - per called the

"Rag - time News". Got rag-time hab-its and I talk that way, I sleep in rag time and I

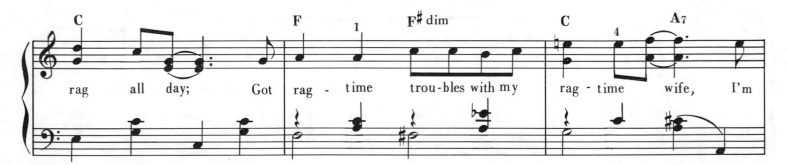

rag all day; Got rag - time trou-bles with my rag - time wife, I'm

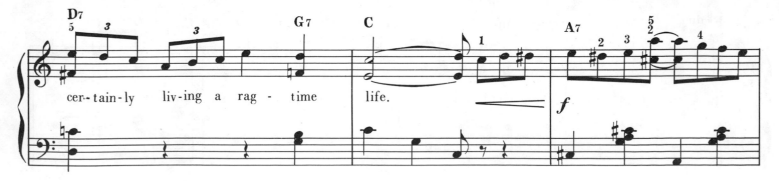

cer--tain-ly liv-ing a rag - time life.

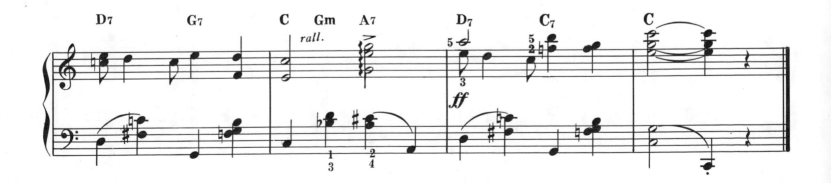

Black and White Rag

Edited by Denes Agay

George Botsford

Moderately lively

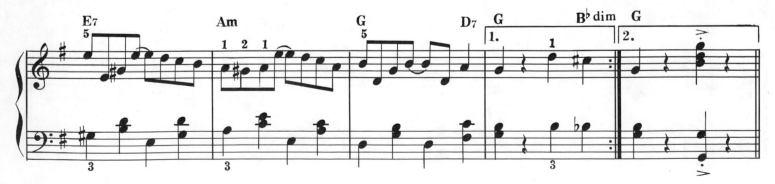

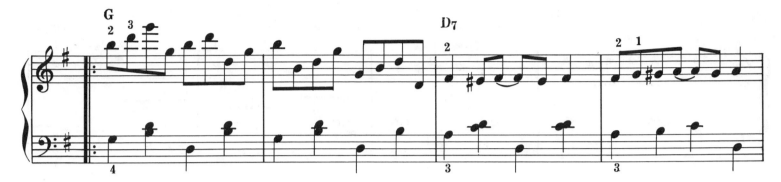

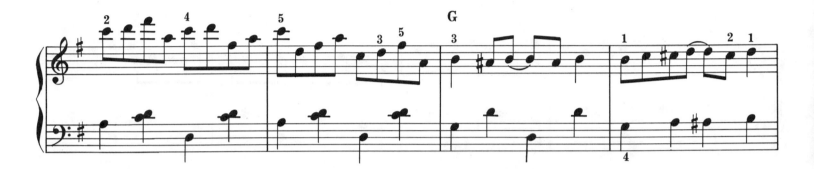

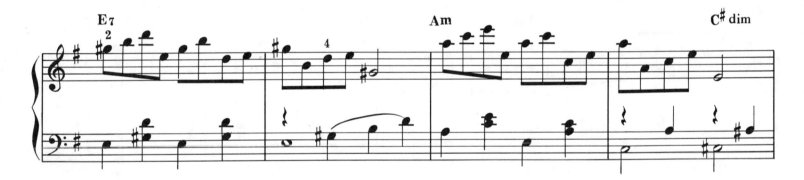

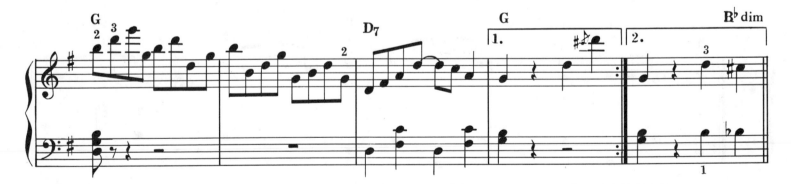

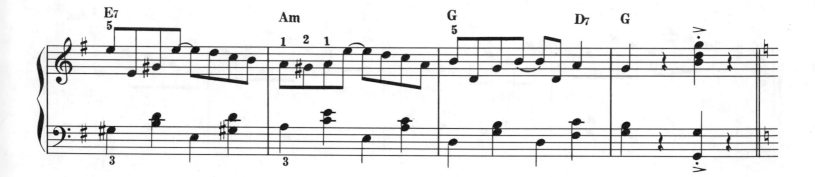

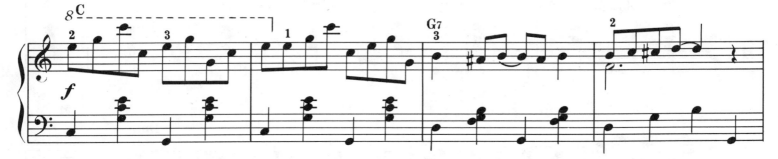

Cotton Bolls

Lively *Tempo di Rag*

Charles Hunter

*Original edition in the key of D♭.

© Yorktown Music Press, Inc. 1974

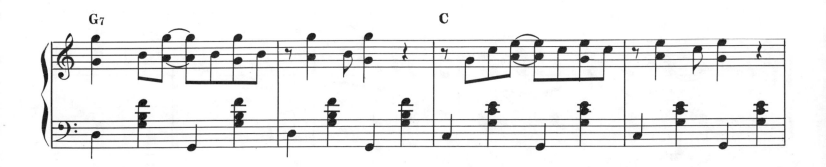

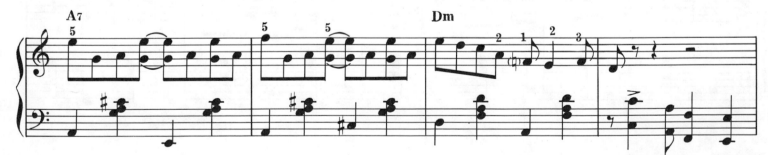

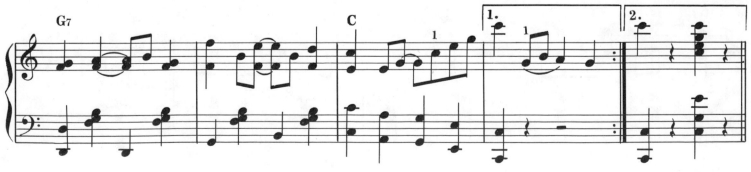

D.C. al Fine

Mandy's Broadway Stroll

Thomas E. Broady

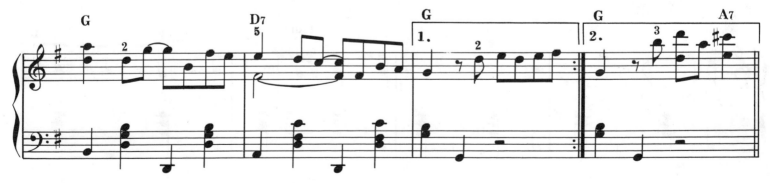

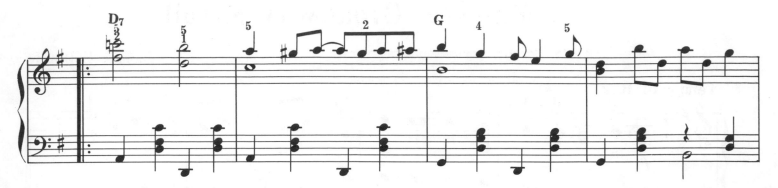

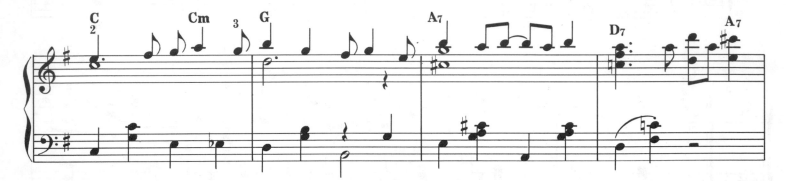

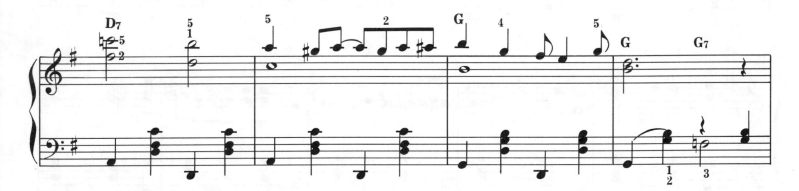

Trio

D.S. al Fine

Classical Rag
"Kyrene"

Edited by Denes Agay

E. J. Stark

Slow two - step tempo

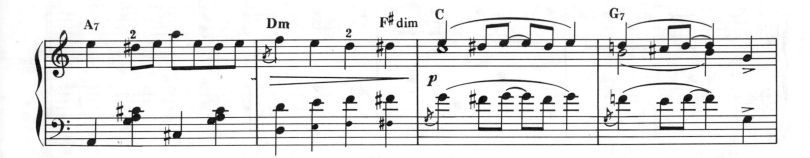

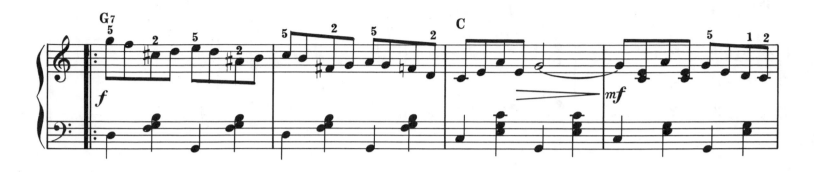

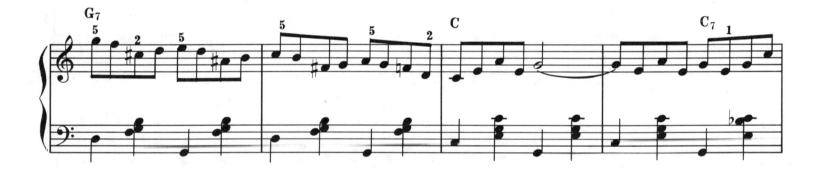

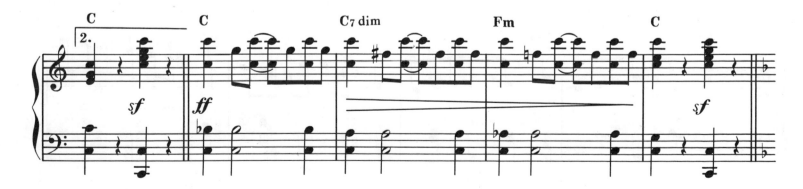

Trio

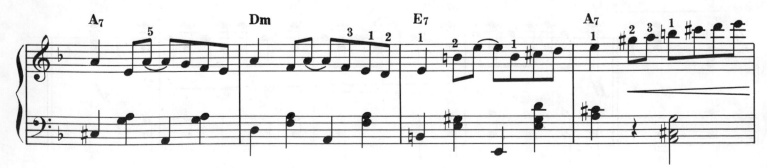

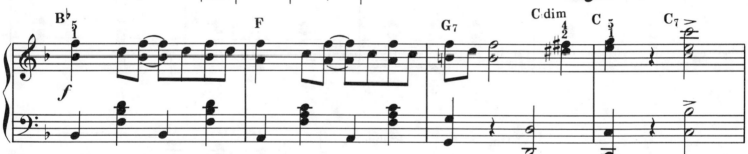

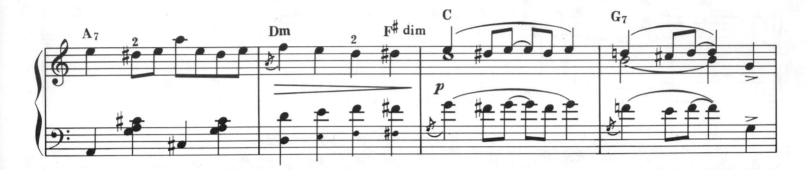

Joplin Gallery

Selected themes
edited by Denes Agay

Scott Joplin

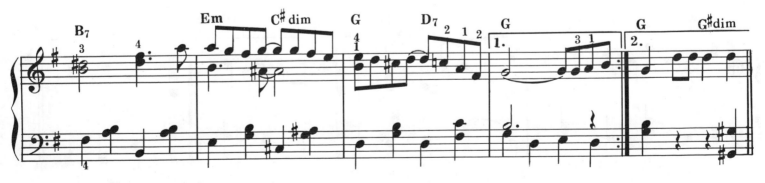

* The three sections of this selection may be played separately or in sequence.

("The Cascades")

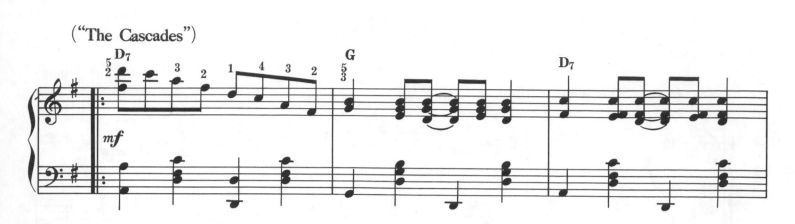

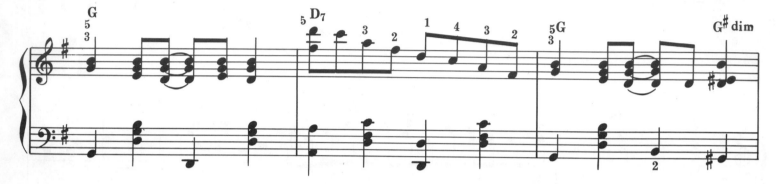

("The Strenuous Life")

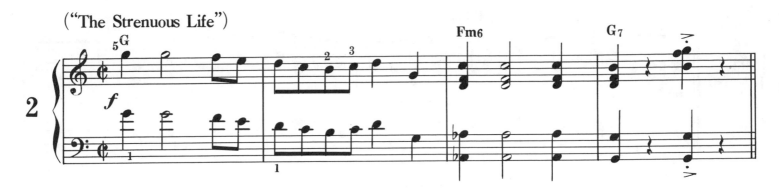

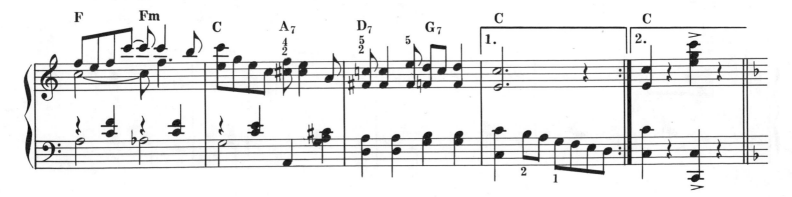

("Palm Leaf Rag")

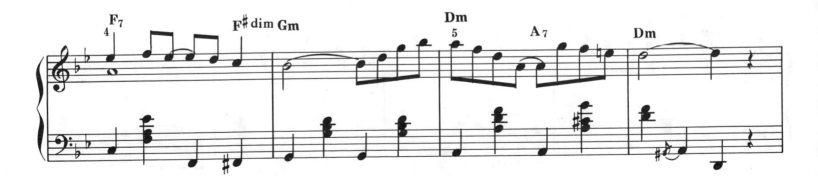

("Peacherine Rag")

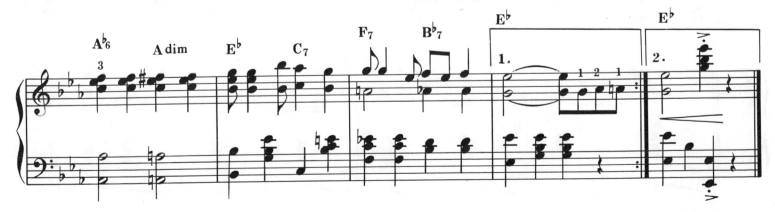

Peaches and Cream

Edited by Denes Agay

Percy Wenrich

Ragtime tempo (Not fast)

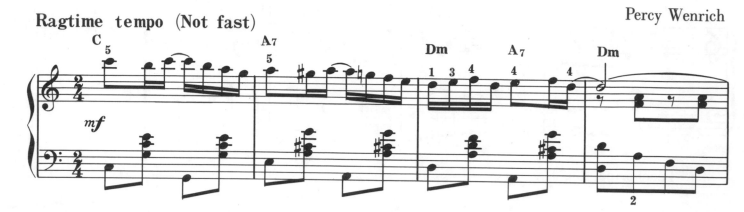

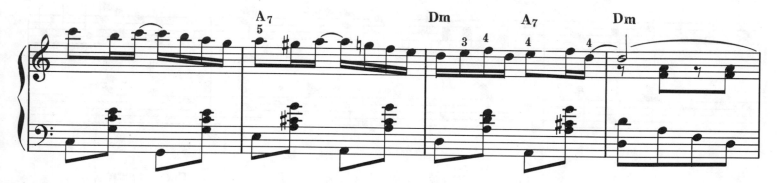

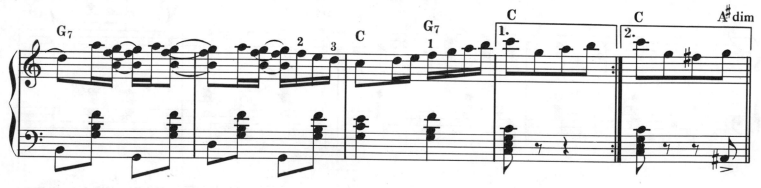

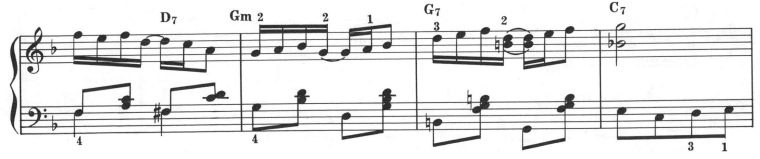

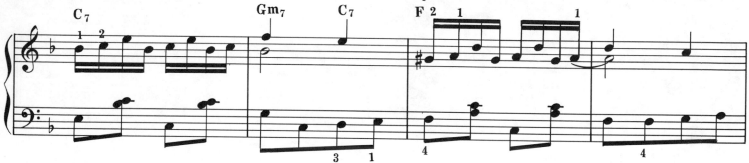

The St. Louis Rag

Tom Turpin

Allegretto

44

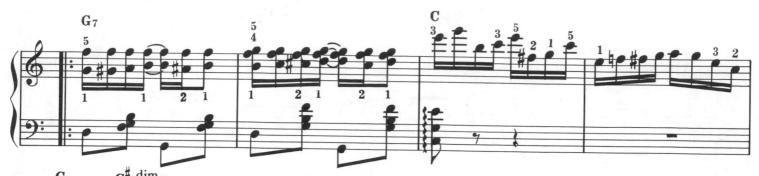

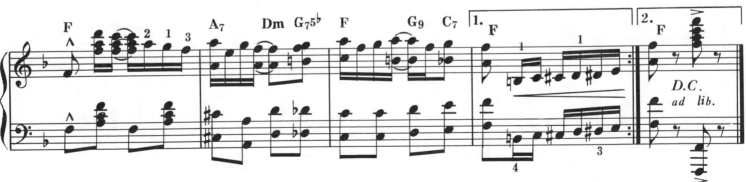

Calico Rag

Two-Step

Lee B. Grabbe

Moderate rag tempo

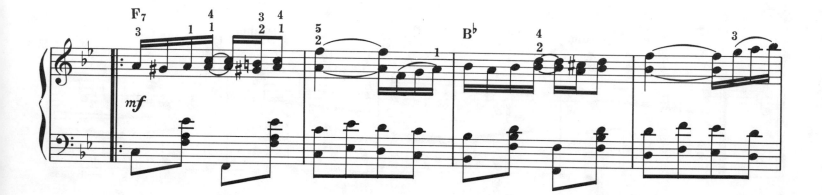

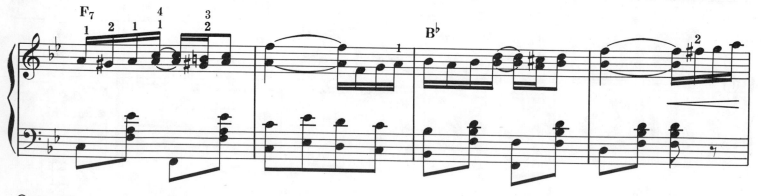

47

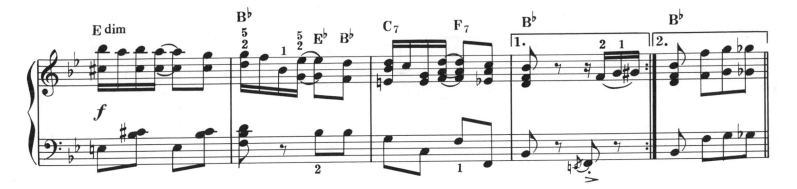

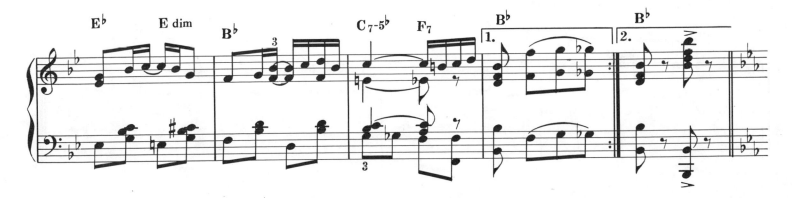

Trio

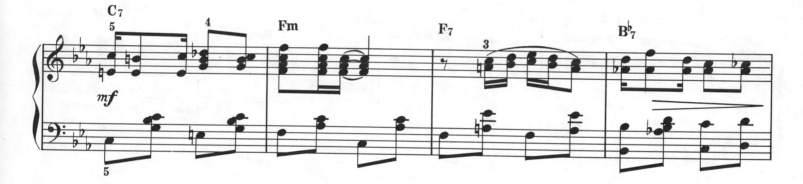

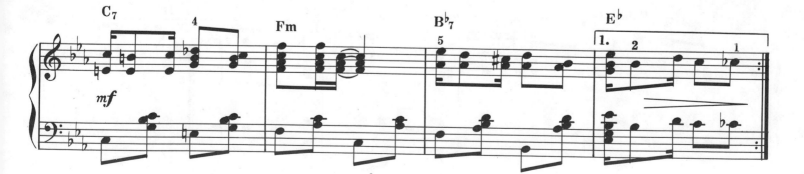

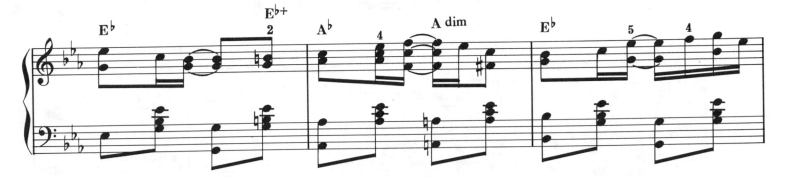

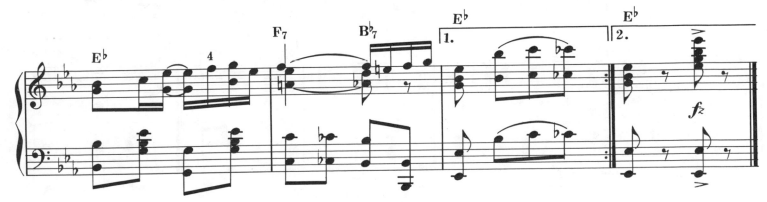

The Sycamore
A Concert Rag

Scott Joplin

"Ragtime" march tempo

51

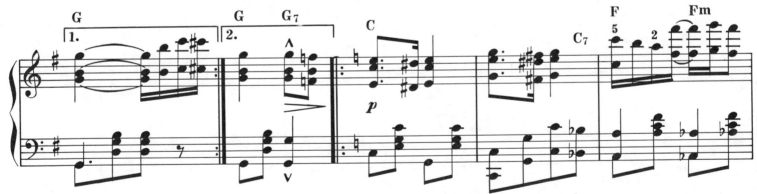

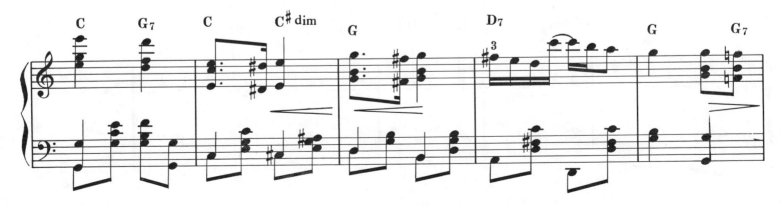

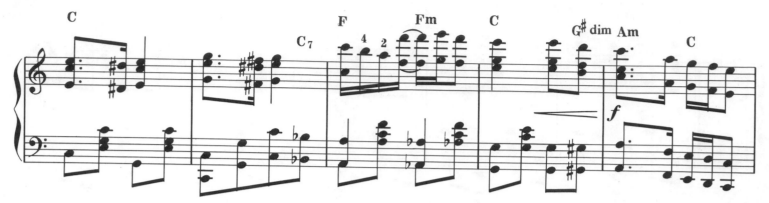

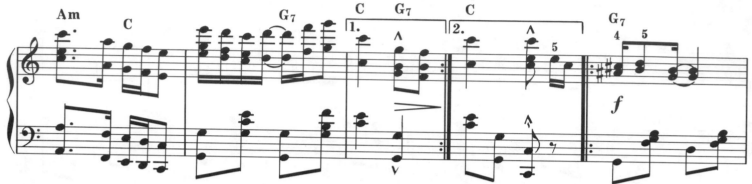

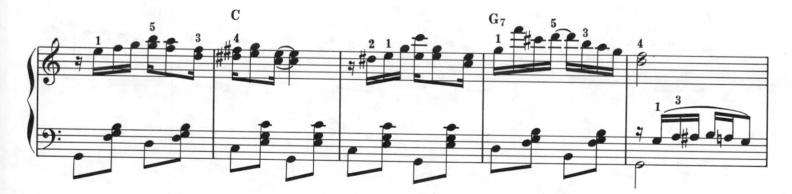

Kansas City Rag

James Scott

Not too fast

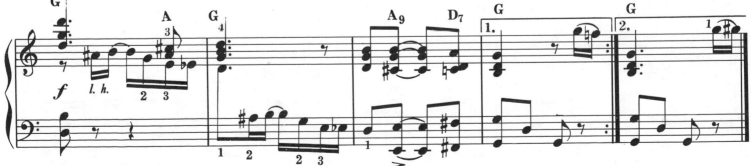

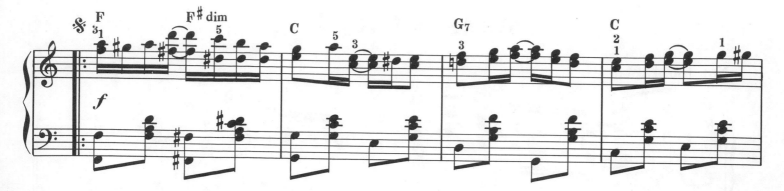

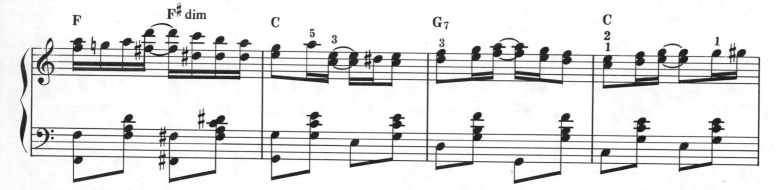

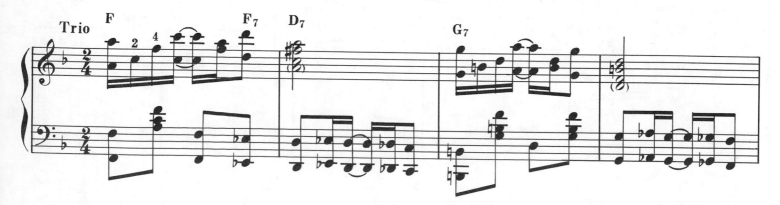

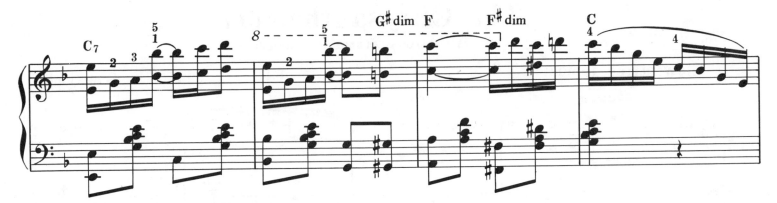

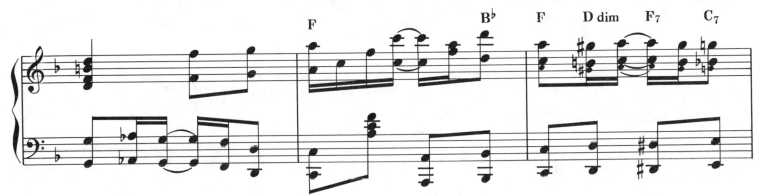

D.S. al Fine

The Chrysanthemum

An Afro-American Intermezzo

Scott Joplin

Slow march tempo

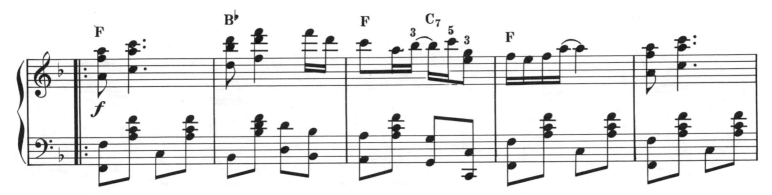

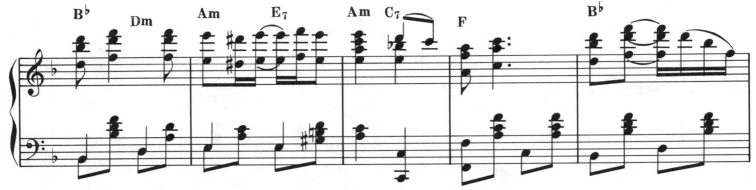

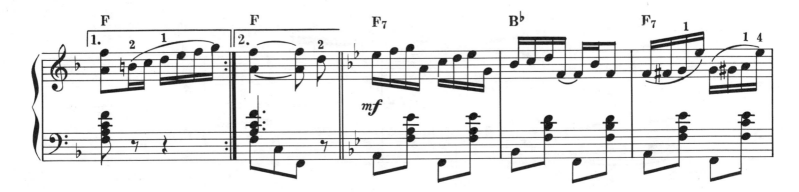

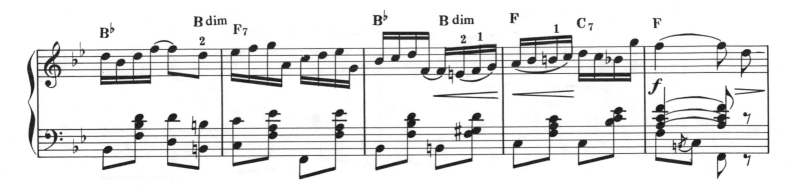

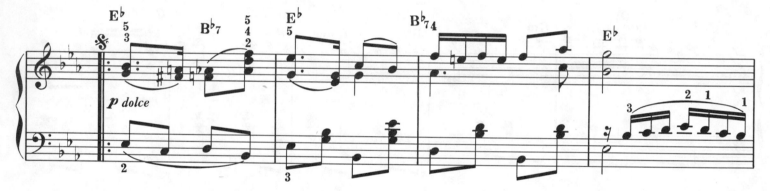

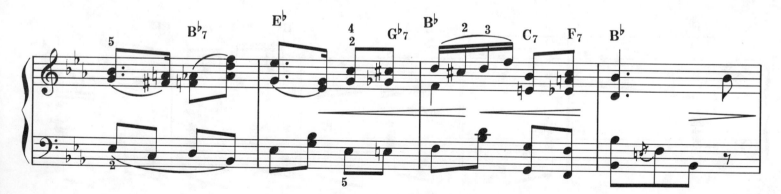

Fine

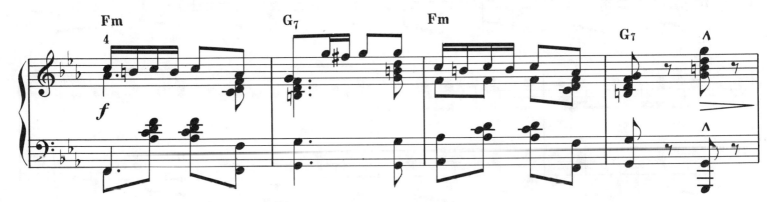

Repeat from 𝄋 with second ending

Bohemia

Rag

Joseph F. Lamb

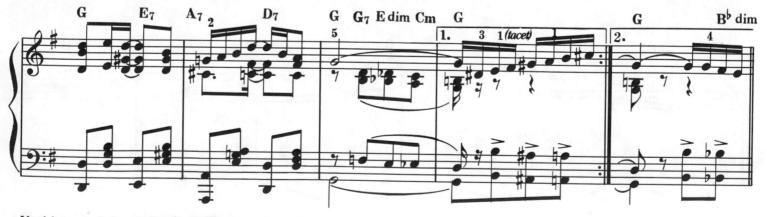

62

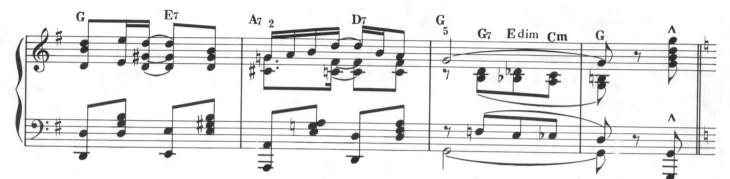

63

Maple Leaf Rag

Tempo di Marcia

Scott Joplin

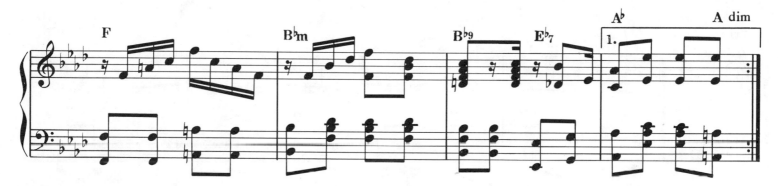

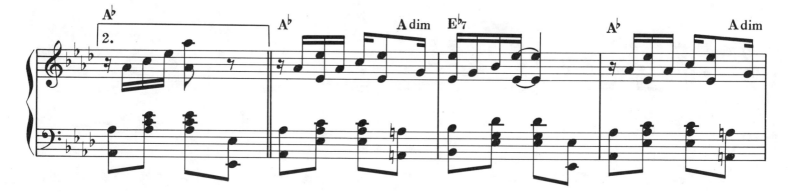

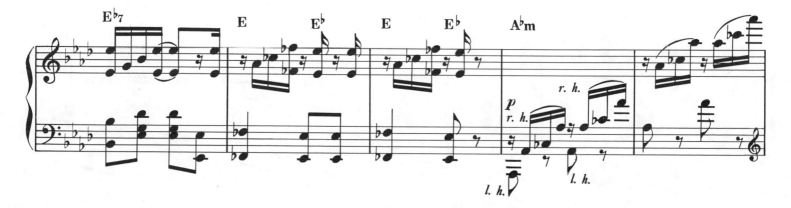

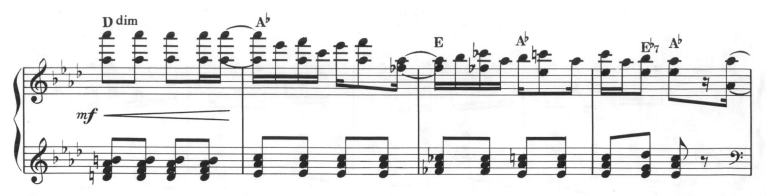

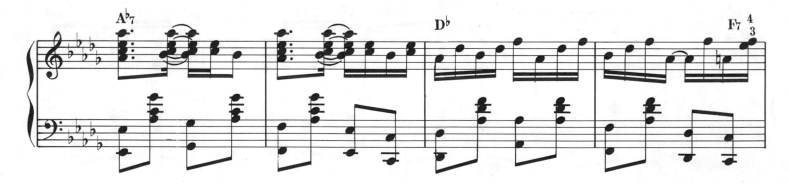

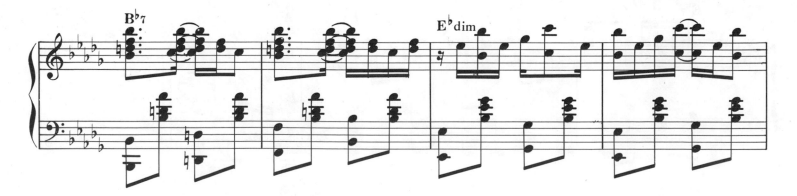

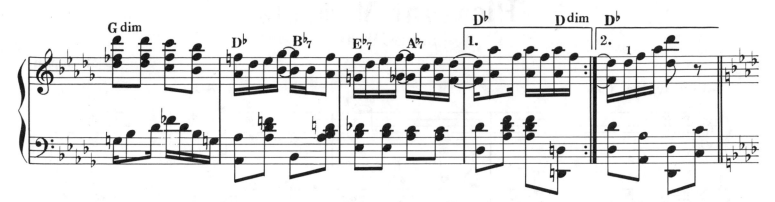

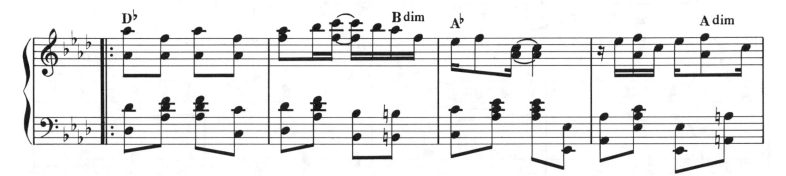

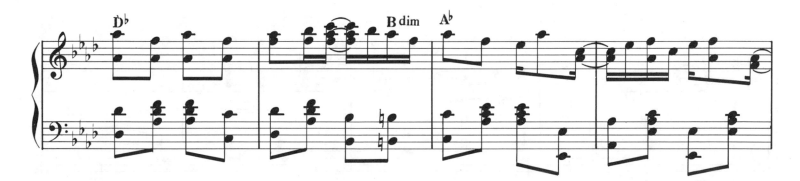

Pleasant Moments

Ragtime Waltz

Scott Joplin

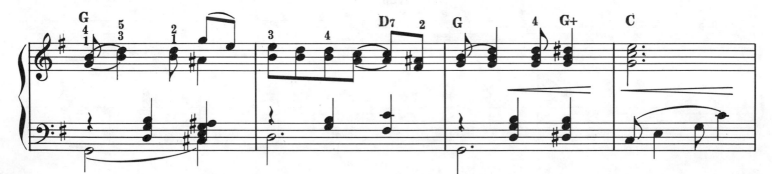

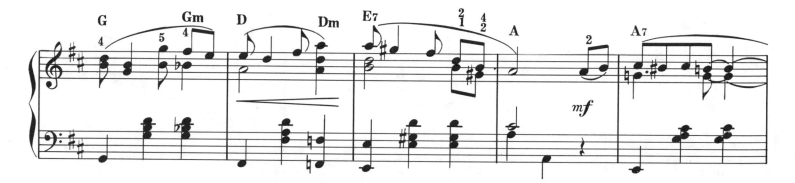

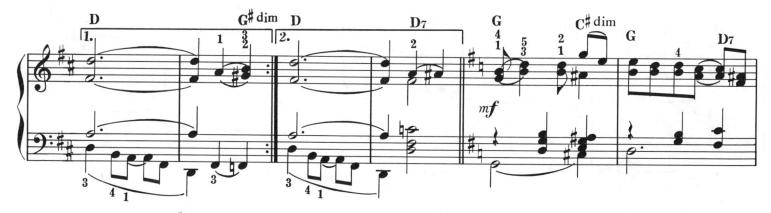

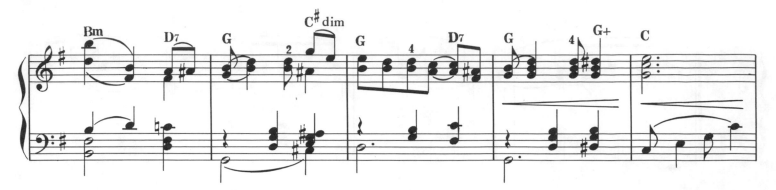

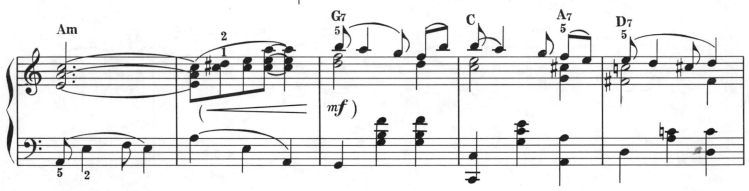

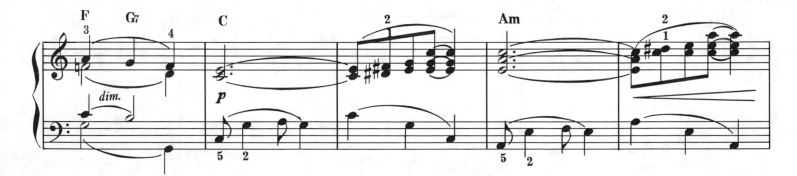

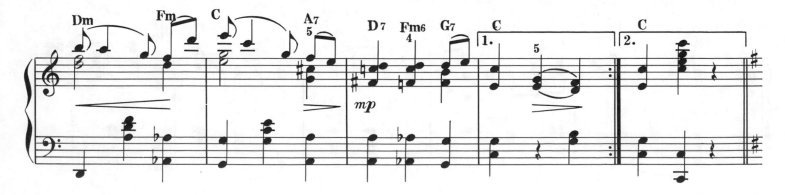

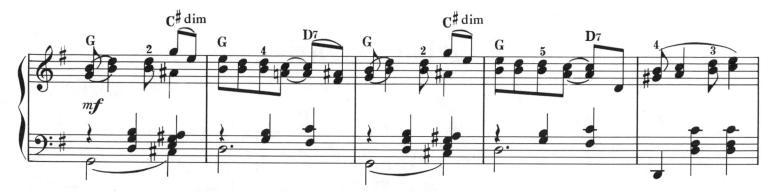

Ragtime Nightingale

Joseph F. Lamb

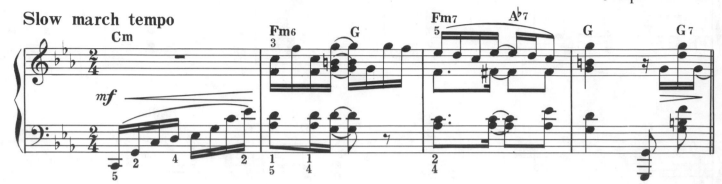

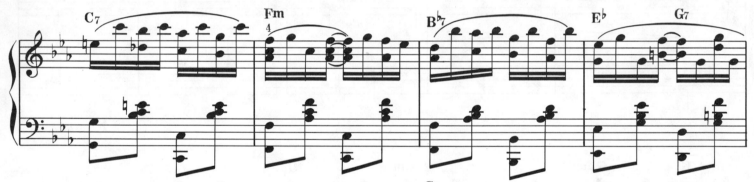

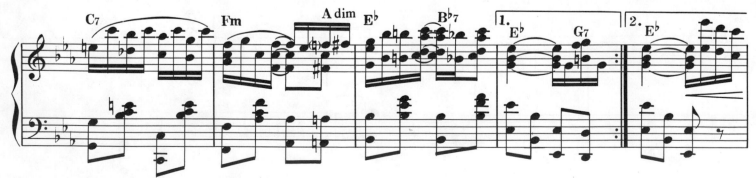

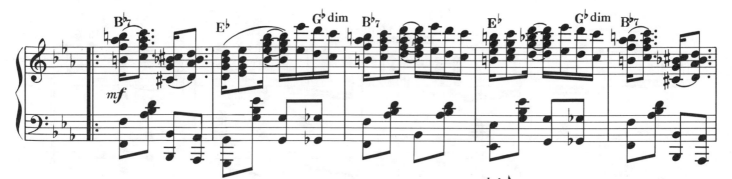

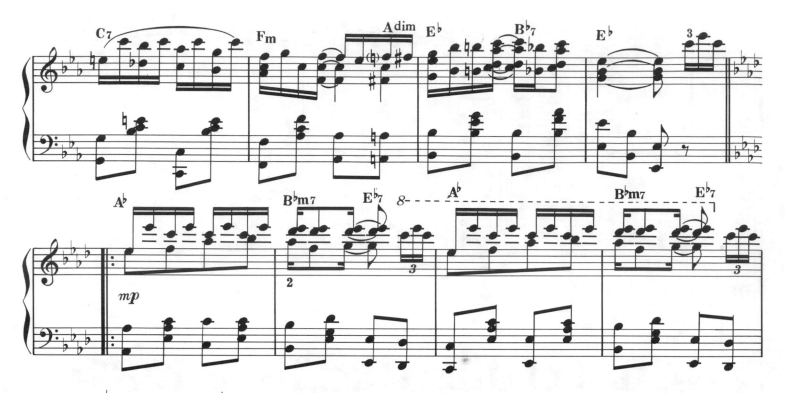

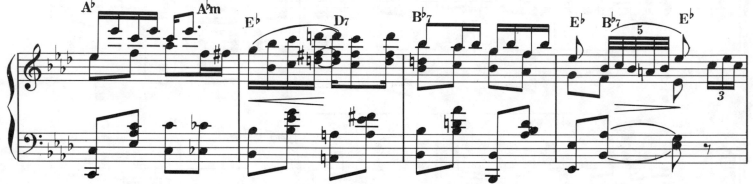

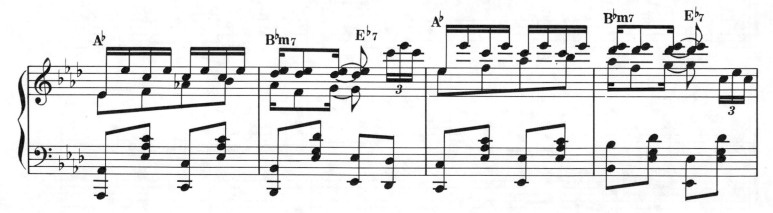

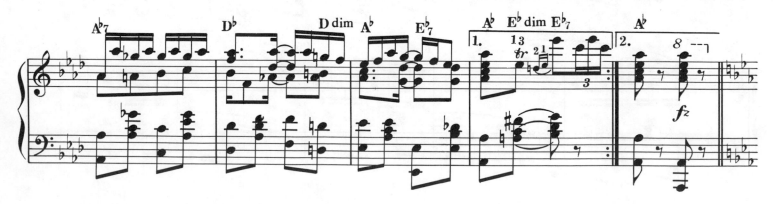

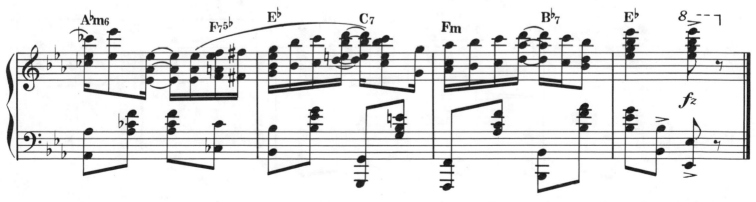

Frog Legs Rag

James Scott

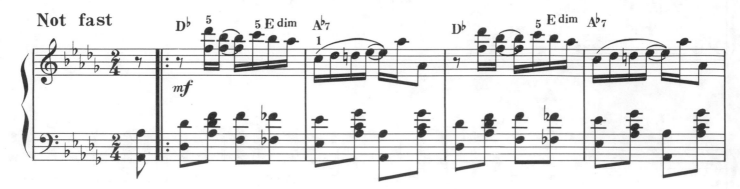

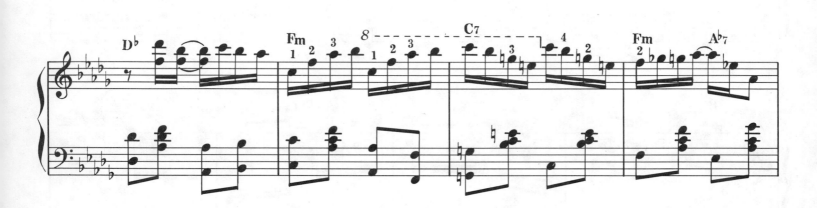

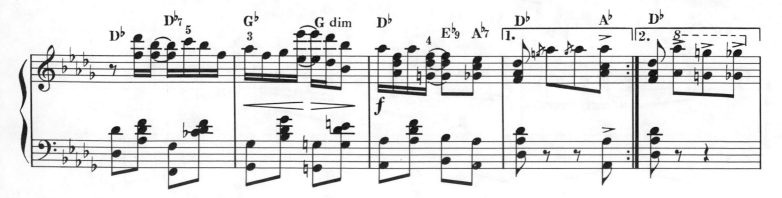

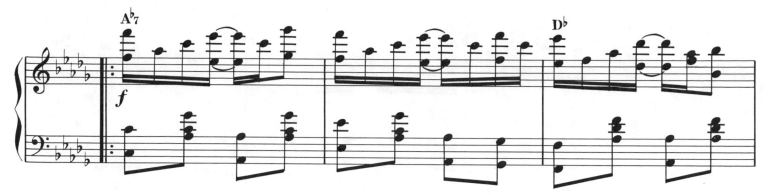

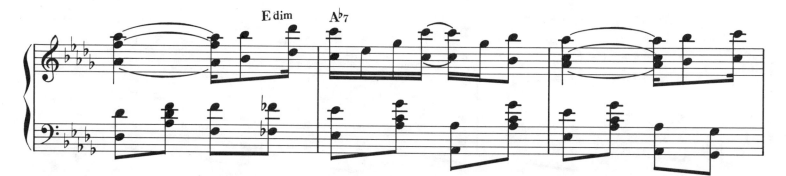

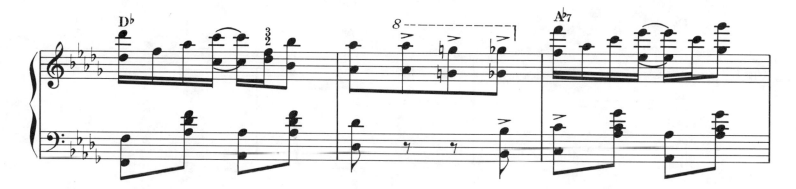

78

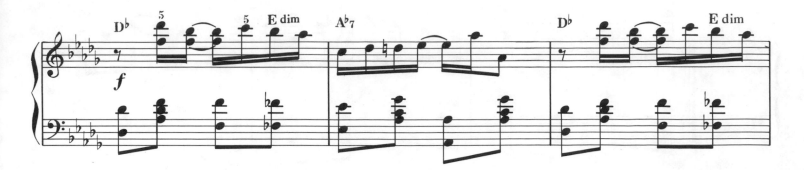

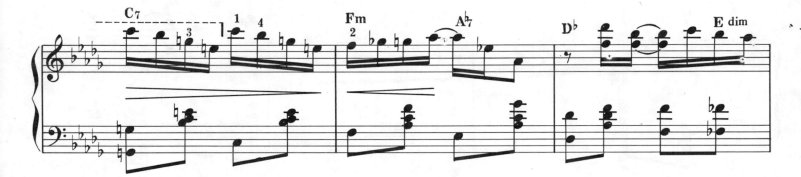

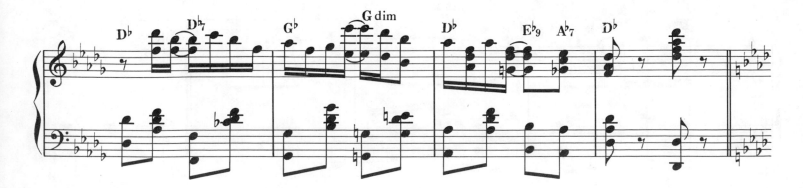

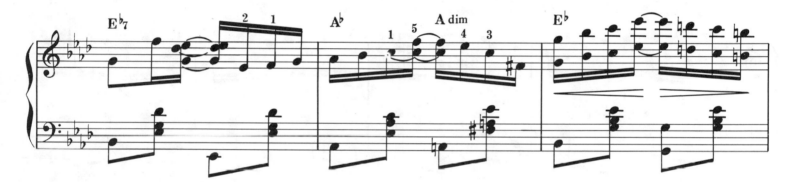

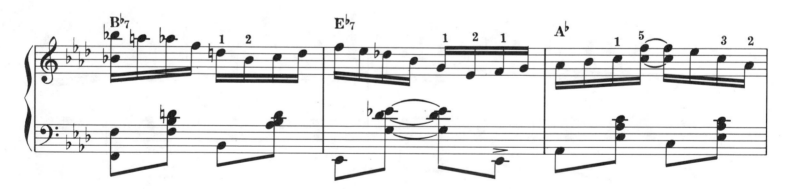

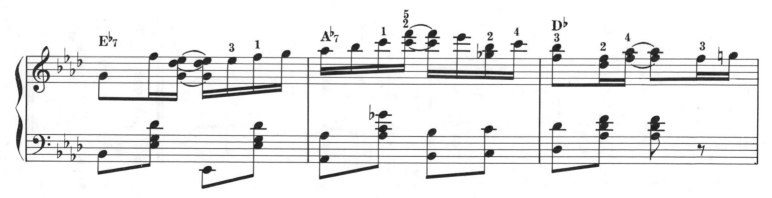

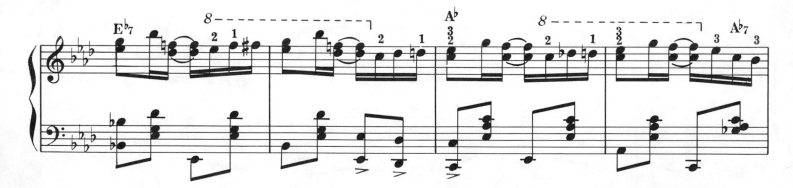

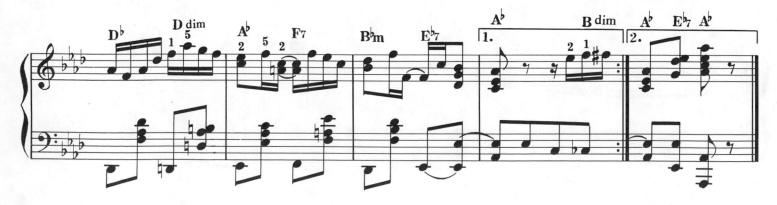